THE GENTLE GIANT

(Caring for the Newfoundland Dog)

by

Margaret Brazear

TABLE OF CONTENTS

THE GENTLE GIANT
NEWFOUNDLAND FACTS
NEWFOUNDLAND GROOMING
LIFESPAN
NEWFOUNDLAND PUPPIES
NEWFOUNDLAND PUPPY CARE
NEWFOUNDLAND BREED STANDARD
BOATSWAIN, LORD BYRON'S NEWFIE
MY GRANDEST PUP
NEWFOUNDLAND DOG STORIES
SEAMAN THE NEWFIE EXPLORER
GANDER, THE BRAVEST NEWFIE
NEWFOUNDLAND HISTORY
NEWFOUNDLAND TRAINING
HOUSETRAINING
POSITIVE DOG TRAINING
NEWFOUNDLAND BREEDERS
HOW TO AVOID PUPPY FARMERS
HOW TO FIND GOOD NEWFIE BREEDERS
CHOOSING A PUPPY
THINGS TO BEWARE OF
NEWFOUNDLAND HEALTH
CANINE PARVOVIRUS
CANINE HEPATITIS
LEPTOSPIROSIS (Weil's Disease)
CANINE DISTEMPER - HARD PAD
KENNEL COUGH
CANINE RABIES
HIP DYSPLASIA
ELBOW DYSPLASIA
SUBVALVULAR AORTIC STENOSIS
CANINE BLOAT AKA GASTRIC TORSION
CANINE ARTHRITIS
DOG HYDROTHERAPY
HEATSTROKE
LIVER CAKE
LIVESTOCK GUARDIAN DOGS

THE GENTLE GIANT

Newfoundland Dogs, universally known as the gentle giants, the aristocrat among dogs. They are certainly the gentle giants, so sweet natured it is easy to forget that they are in fact, dogs.

I have lost count of the number of times I have received emails asking about Newfoundland Dogs, from people who really, really want to get one. I always start by telling them their bad points, though these are not bad points to me, just a minor inconvenience.

The first thing to remember is that the majority of them drool! I have heard of newfies who do not do this, but mine do, and in vast quantities. Unfortunately, it is not something you will know until they get older. They drool on my clothes when they lay their heads on my knee, they shake their heads and I get little ribbons all over the walls, the cupboards, the furniture. There is nothing you can do about this, so you have to learn to live with it. I always have kitchen roll with me, just in case.

Some people have a serious aversion to dog drool, and if that is you, forget the very idea of owning a newfie. Sometimes they want to go say hello to people who have made the mistake of talking to them from a distance, and I can see they are dressed for an occasion and have to hold them back.

Any other bad points? That depends on your point of view. Newfoundland dogs are excessively hairy and will leave fur everywhere, on your carpet, on your cupboard handles, in your dishwasher, upstairs even if they never go there. Their fur is waterproof and it will stick to absolutely everything. I have found that only a wool carpet will do, as it is impossible to get the hairs off anything else.

The one thing I have found which puts most people off is when they realise just how big they will be. My Ferdie is 80kg, about 180lbs. Very often, after everything I have told them about their wonderful nature, people will say: "I didn't realise they got *that* big!"

When you decide to buy a Newfoundland dog, you are buying a giant breed. He is going to be enormous! Some have been known to grow to the size of a small Shetland pony - are you prepared to have a Shetland pony in your house?

They are a breed which will bond with their person and will be miserable without that person. Remember that when you consider sharing your life with one of these magnificent creatures - it will be for life, more binding than a marriage.

I often have people asking if I have a really big house. Well, I just don't have a lot of furniture.

If you have fallen in love with the idea of a newfie, if you want all the facts about them, you have come to the right place.

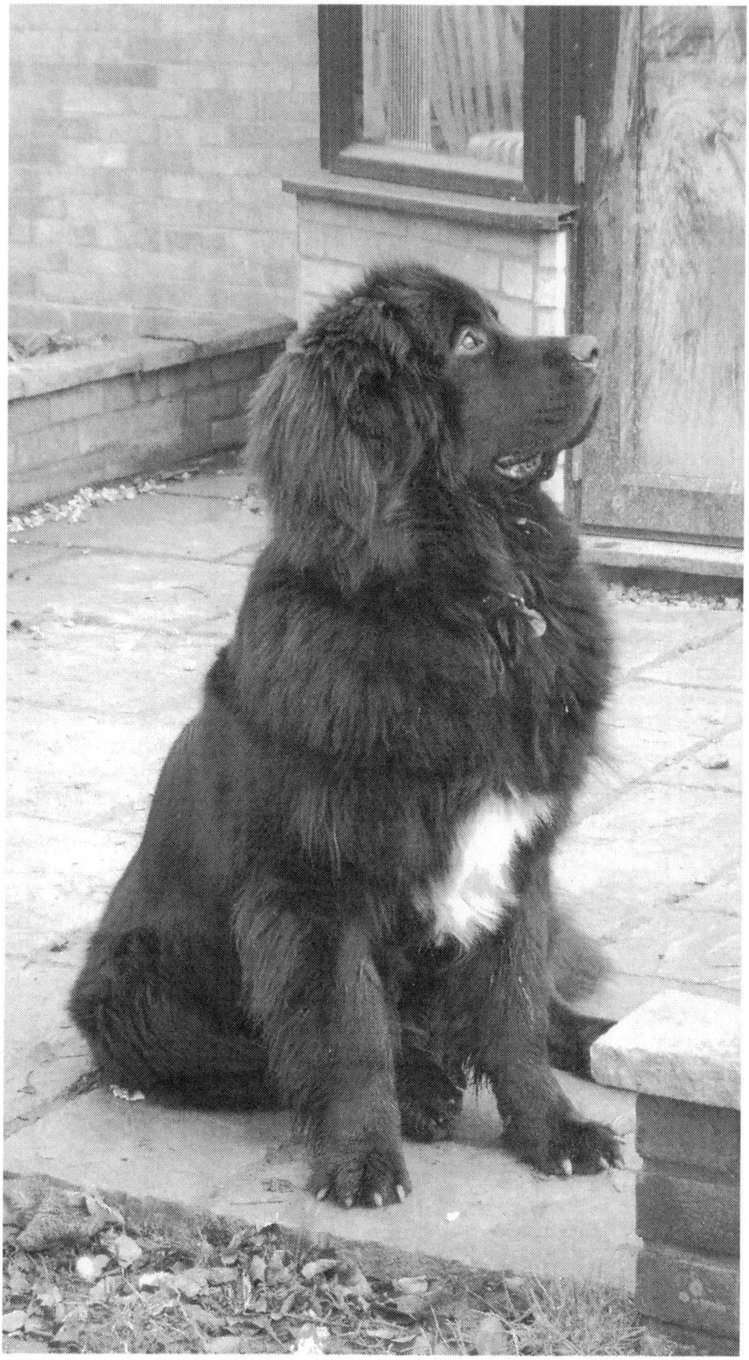

NEWFIE FACTS

What is the Newfoundland dog really like? They are well known for their gentle nature, and their special affinity with children, so much so that in Victorian times wealthy people would buy a newfie as a sort of nanny dog, to protect their children. The dog Nana, featured in the original Peter Pan novel, was based upon a landseer Newfoundland named Luath, belonging to the book's author, J.M. Barrie. It is unfortunate that in plays and films he tends to pop up as either a St Bernard or an Old English Sheepdog.

Despite their wonderful nature, it is important to realise that as a puppy they can easily knock down a young child and supervision must be maintained. They can get over excited, like any puppy, and damage can easily be done unintentionally.

Newfoundlands are people dogs. They will never do well away from their family, outside in a kennel. They will follow you about all over the house, will be in front of the cooker when you are trying to cook, will be next to you when you are sitting at your desk. And they love to lean on people! This can be a very endearing trait, but remember how heavy they are when they decide to lean against someone who is a bit fragile.

They also like to give a paw, and this is not really something that you want to encourage. My arms used to be covered in bruises, simply where Ferdie had given me his paw and I once went to a job interview with a long and vivid scratch down the side of my face, from Ferdie's affectionate paw giving.

These dogs drink vast amounts of water and they like to sleep outside in the evenings, especially in the summer. They will get very frustrated if they cannot do this, so a home with no garden is definitely unsuitable.

Newfoundland dogs will normally need little in the way of loose leash training, as it is not in their nature to pull on the lead. Pulling on a lead is usually a sign that the dog can smell prey - not that he wants to be in charge of the walk as these pack leader enthusiasts would have it. Newfies have very little, if any prey drive. If they pull at all it is because they want to get on with it, they are excited.

However, every dog is different and they can still pull you along if they see something they want, so a certain amount of training is essential. Someone told me once that I must be strong to hold the two of them while we were talking. Well, they are each heavier than me and if they wanted to go, strength would not hold them back.

Basic Training is essential, and it is important to know the breed traits of these beautiful dogs to achieve that. Please pay particular attention to the training pages of this book.

These dogs need very little exercise, especially when they are growing. They are not a dog who is going to go jogging with you, or run along beside a cycle. They are quite happy to sleep all day, if you let them, but that is not a good idea. They need socialisation, and early socialisation is essential.

You may have noticed that people with newfies rarely have just one. Most have two, some have more than two. I had someone asked me once if they come in pairs! My reason for having two is simple - Ferdie needed someone his own size to play with. This breed loves other dogs, provided they have been introduced to them early, and they play best with dogs their own size. You will not see many of those. My two are devoted to each other, they do not enjoy going for walks without each other and they lie on the floor licking each other's noses! The best thing I ever did for Ferdie was to get Joshua.

I lost my Joshua at a young age and Ferdie was so depressed, I really thought I would lose him too. I was so lucky that their breeder was looking for a pet home for Diva and after a week of ignoring each other, they began to play. He is not in love with her, as he was with Joshua, but they get on and play together nicely.

GROOMING

Grooming a Newfoundland Dog is a major occupation. I actually came across a dog information website that stated that a newfie only needs an occasional brush! Yeah, right! If you don't want to have to cut out matts from all over the body, his coat needs a lot of work.

A blaster or dog hair dryer is the best thing to remove all the winter coat when it starts to shed, but not every dog will take to it. Ferdie loves the thing and Diva, having been a show dog, is perfectly fine, but the first time Joshua saw it he ran away and hid in the cupboard. I never could use it on him as he was terrified.

A comb is much more efficient for getting their fur out than a brush, even though it will take a long time. Christy's do a butter comb which I haven't used but I have something similar. The prongs spin round so it doesn't get stuck and pull the fur.

These dogs are very easily frightened and if you hurt them once, like pulling their fur by accident, the chances are they are not going to let you near them a second time.

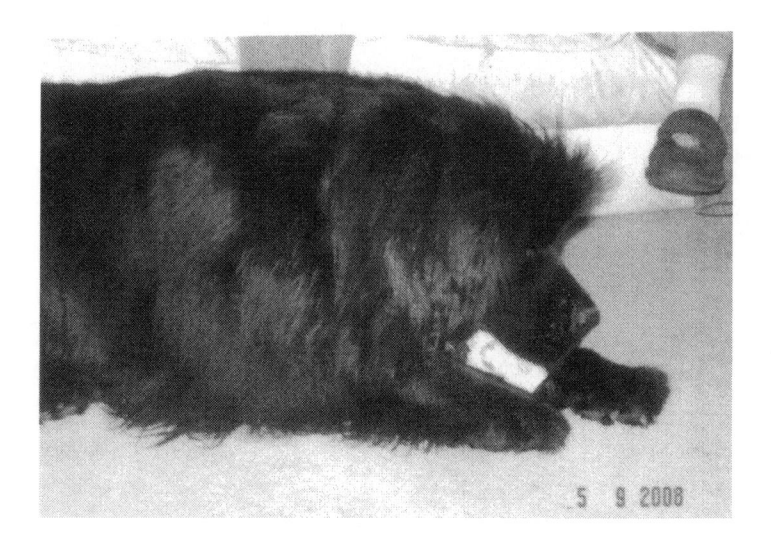

LIFESPAN

What pleased me the most when I started my research, is that their lifespan is much longer than most other giant breeds. Their average lifespan is between twelve and fourteen years, the same as any other large dog breed, whereas a lot of giant dogs do not live to be more than 9 or 10 years old. St Bernards have an average lifespan of only 5 to 7 years, which is heartbreaking.

With the right food and care, you can look forward to having your newfie with you for a very long time.

I started my search when I lost my golden retriever at the age of fourteen. I had always wanted a giant breed but I was under the impression that they all had a short lifespan. I looked at loads on the internet and was thrilled to find that newfies are the exception. There are some others, but they are mostly livestock guardians who are really not suitable pets.

I emailed the Newfoundland Club and was told that it was correct and that they had one who was fifteen.

Last year I met a lady who has had the breed all her life and would never have anything else. We meet at least once a week so that the dogs can all play together, and four of them are a magnificent sight. People do stop and stare, ask lots of questions, some the same as we have heard many times, but they do make an impression.

NEWFIE PUPPIES

Is there anything more delightful on this planet than a puppy dog? Newfoundland puppies are no exception to the cute and cuddly rule, but they will not stay that way for long!

Newfoundland puppies, along with other giant breeds, grow five times faster than any other dog breed. In fact, your puppy will reach two thirds of his adult size by the time he is eight months old!

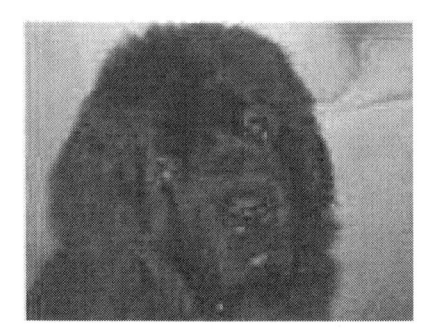

But he still wants to be a puppy and will want to run up and say hello to everybody he meets. I have had to explain on many occasions that he is only a puppy, as people raise their eyebrows sceptically. At eight months, he will most probably be bigger than a full grown Labrador!

He is going to want to charge about the place, just like any other puppy, but he can knock over all your ornaments, even pull things out of your bookshelves, and if he decides to chew the furniture, you can be sure it will not be a few scratches.

When Ferdie was a puppy, he chewed through four dining chairs, an office chair, two mobile phones, seven tv remote controls and he made a major hole in a breezeblock wall! He used to love to drag the office chair, with me on it, across the laminated flooring.

This is the picture sent to me by Ferdie's breeder when I enquired. He is six weeks old in this picture, and as you can see, he is already bigger than the bucket.

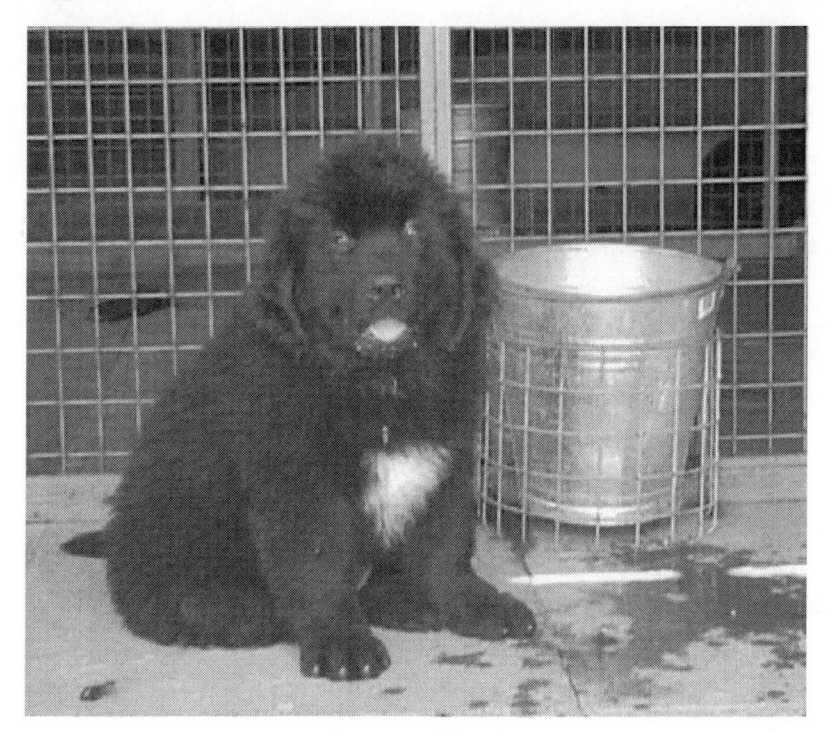

There will not be much that he cannot reach.

A Newfoundland puppy is an extremely affectionate dog. He will want to be with you, wherever you are, so get into the habit of looking down before you move. Chances are he will be right there, under your feet.

They love cuddles, they love kisses, and they love to please. They are fairly easy to housetrain, given the right guidance, as they are extremely intelligent and do get the message very quickly. However, any harsh treatment will set your puppy back by months.

Along with most giant dogs, they hate to be shouted at. It fills them with fear and if it comes from the person they have learned to trust, that trust will be hard to regain.

A newfie has been bred for centuries to work on his own initiative. You cannot expect him to think of you as anything other than an equal and a friend. But he will look up to you as the one with the resources. You are the one who provides the food, the games, the walks and he will look to you for everything good in his life.

Basic puppy training for a Newfoundland puppy is really not difficult, but it is an ongoing thing and it is time consuming.

All puppies are hard work. Think carefully, as you would before deciding to have a baby. You will have to devote much of your time to this puppy for quite a few months to come, so try to think past the cute and cuddly puppy thoughts, and realise that raising a puppy, any puppy, is hard work.

Newfoundland puppies can be even harder work. They have very special needs in puppy care and if you ignore those basic needs, you will let yourself in for a lot of heartache and your dog will suffer for it.

Finding a reputable breeder is the most important thing when it comes to choosing a puppy. I cannot stress enough the importance of choosing your puppy wisely.

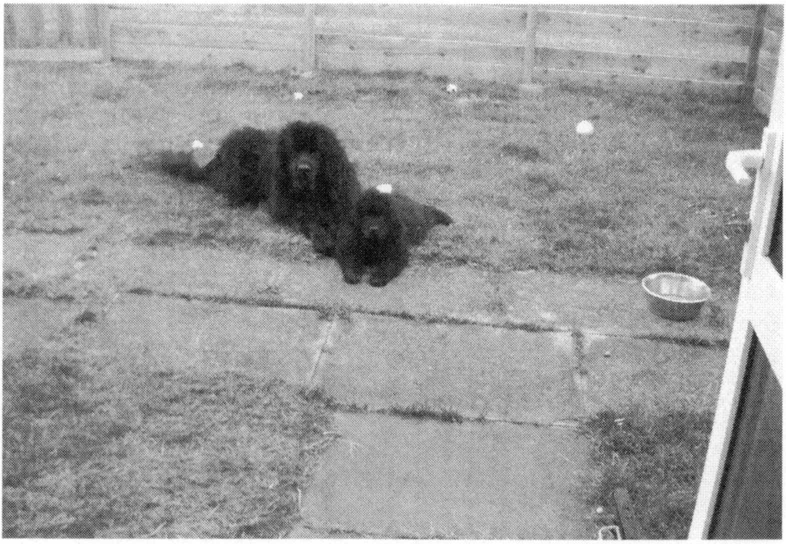

NEWFOUNDLAND PUPPY CARE

A Newfoundland puppy is very delicate. It is no simple task to care for their growing joints and sometimes it is quite upsetting, when you see them wanting to play and run and you have to step in and stop them.

Because they grow so fast, any strain on their joints can cause permanent damage. You must keep them at a slow walking pace when they are very young, as tempting as it is to let them have fun like any other puppy.

The rule for walking is five minutes per day per month of their lives. So, a three month old puppy should have no longer than a fifteen minute walk per day. This can be increased as they get a little older, but care should be taken that they do not run for more than a few minutes.

You may find yourself disagreeing with well meaning but interfering people who tell you that he is fine to run - he is a puppy. I remember having an argument with the owner of a small terrier who told me that my puppy needed to be able to run. You cannot compare a terrier to a giant breed; you must learn to know that you know best, and walk away. Your Newfoundland puppy will suffer if you do not.

It is a fact of life that when you are out with a puppy, everybody assumes you need their advice - you don't. You will also find that a vast majority of dog owners firmly believe that a big dog must needs loads of exercise. Again, this is a mistake, especially whilst your puppy is growing.

You absolutely must not let him climb stairs, go down stairs, or jump into the car. This last may just get him into the habit of waiting to be lifted in, which you will not want when he is full grown! It is best to start off with a dog ramp, teach him to walk up it so that later on he is happy to do so.

Do think carefully about the cost of newfoundland food. You cannot feed a dog like this on cheap stuff from the supermarket. They need very special large or giant breed puppy food, in order that their delicate bones and joints grow properly. Look carefully at the ingredients: you don't want anything that is full of fillers and cereals and the meat or fish content needs to be the first ingredient listed. These foods are expensive, but they are what your puppy needs.

You may also find that the first time you take your puppy out on his lead, he will get as far as next door and lie down! This is very much a newfie trait and one you need to take gently, a little further every day until he is happy.

Newfoundland dogs, even adult ones, have a tendency to suddenly lie down and refuse to move. Ferdie used to do it all the time and still does on occasion, so do not decide to take him out before you have to be somewhere! You need lots of time, just in case.

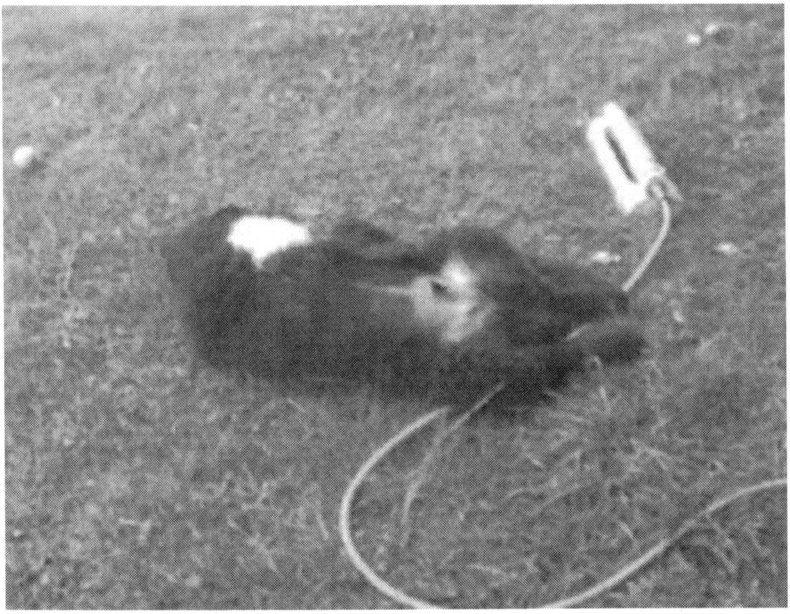

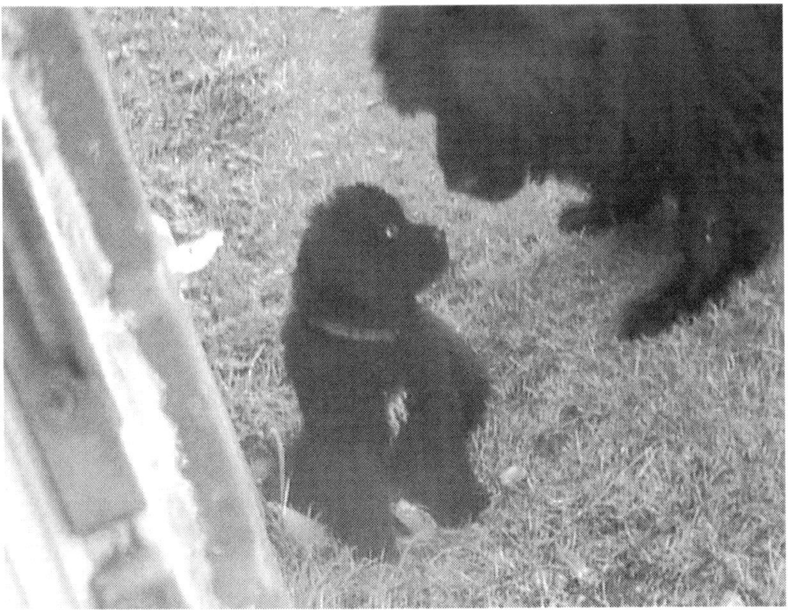

NEWFOUNDLAND BREED STANDARD

The accepted colours in the United Kingdom for the Newfoundland dog breed are black, with or without a white blaze, brown or bronze and white and black, which colour is also known as Landseer.

The black and white newfoundland got his name from Sir Edwin Landseer, who painted many pictures of the black and white giant dog.

The Landseer is mostly white, usually with black hind quarters. The black dog sometimes has white paws, which is also acceptable, and I have seen one with the tip of his tail in white. This is very attractive, but I don't know how well he would do in the showring.

People usually think of the newfie as being black and I once had an interesting conversation with someone who thought that a well known local newfie must be a cross breed because he was brown! I put him straight of course.

Be very aware of people trying to sell a "rare" newfoundland dog. I saw an ad on the internet last year for landseer newfoundland puppies, very rare colour, £1800. That is well above the price of a good pedigree puppy and the puppies were brown and white, not black and white.

I am told that this colour is the result of crossing a landseer (black and white) newfie with a brown one. The colour is not accepted by the Kennel Clubs so, far from being rare, it is in fact an inferior colour.

Of course, if you have no interest in showing and do not mind the unacceptable colour, there is nothing wrong with the dog, but it is doubtful that this sort of "breeder" will have carried out any health tests.

This sort of rarity should be a lot cheaper, not more expensive.

The **American Kennel Club** also includes grey in its breed standard. I have never seen a grey newfoundland dog, they are not something one is likely to find in the United Kingdom.

However, should you be offered a grey Newfie as a rare colour in the UK, take note. This colour is not accepted as breed standard by the **UK Kennel Club.**

LORD BYRON'S NEWFOUNDLAND DOG, BOATSWAIN

Boatswain Lord Byron's beloved newfoundland dog died at the age of only five years after contracting rabies.

The famous poet is reputed to have said at the time: "he expired in a state of madness on the 18th after suffering much, yet retaining all the gentleness of his nature to the last; never attempting to do the least injury to any one near him. I have now lost everything"

The poet is reported to have nursed the dog throughout his illness, without fear of being bitten and contracting the awful disease himself.

Near this Spot are deposited the Remains of one who possessed Beauty without Vanity, Strength without Insolence, Courage without Ferosity, and all the virtues of Man without his Vices. This praise, which would be unmeaning Flattery if inscribed over human Ashes, is but a just tribute to the Memory of BOATSWAIN, a DOG, who was born in Newfoundland May 1803 and died at Newstead Nov. 18, 1808.

> Near this Spot
> are deposited the Remains of one
> who possessed Beauty without Vanity,
> Strength without Insolence,
> Courage without Ferosity,
> and all the virtues of Man without his Vices.
> This praise, which would be unmeaning Flattery
> if inscribed over human Ashes,
> is but a just tribute to the Memory of
> BOATSWAIN, a DOG,
> who was born in Newfoundland May 1803
> and died at Newstead Nov.r 18th 1808.

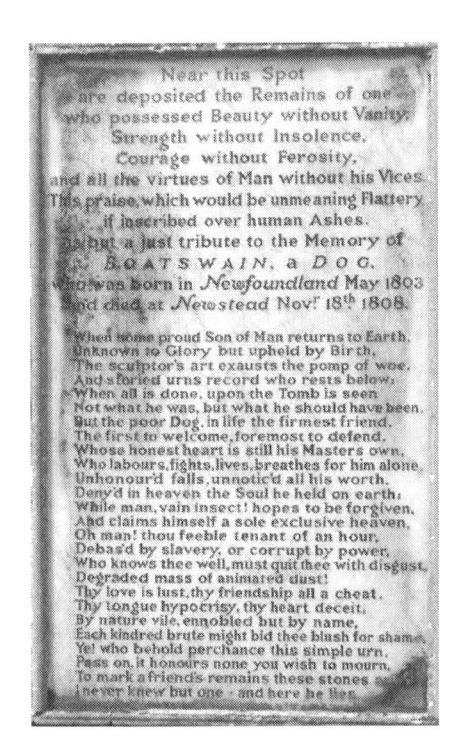

Lord Byron wrote **Epitaph to a Dog** which is inscribed on Boatswain's tomb

When some proud Son of Man returns to Earth,
Unknown by Glory, but upheld by Birth,
The sculptor's art exhausts the pomp of woe,
And storied urns record who rests below.
When all is done, upon the Tomb is seen,
Not what he was, but what he should have been.
But the poor Dog, in life the firmest friend,
The first to welcome, foremost to defend,
Whose honest heart is still his Master's own,
Who labours, fights, lives, breathes for him alone,
Unhonoured falls, unnoticed all his worth,
Denied in heaven the Soul he held on earth -
While man, vain insect! hopes to be forgiven,
And claims himself a sole exclusive heaven.
Oh man! thou feeble tenant of an hour,

Debased by slavery, or corrupt by power -
Who knows thee well must quit thee with disgust,
Degraded mass of animated dust!
Thy love is lust, thy friendship all a cheat,
Thy tongue hypocrisy, thy heart deceit!
By nature vile, ennobled but by name,
Each kindred brute might bid thee blush for shame.
Ye, who perchance behold this simple urn,
Pass on - it honors none you wish to mourn.
To mark a friend's remains these stones arise;
I never knew but one - and here he lies.

In his Will, executed in 1811, Byron instructs that he be buried in the vault with Boatswain. In fact the dog's tomb at Newstead Abbey, is bigger than Byron's own.

MY GRANDEST PUP

<u>MY GRANDEST PUP</u>

(author unknown)

*I'll lend you for a little while
My grandest pup, He said.
For you to love while he's alive
And mourn for when he's dead.
It may be one or twenty years,
Or days or months , you see.
But, will you, till I take him back,
Take care of him for me?
He'll bring her charms to gladden you,
And should his stay be brief,
You'll have treasured memories
As solace for your grief.
I cannot promise he will stay,
Since all from earth return.
But, there are lessons taught on earth
I want this pup to learn.
I've looked the wide world over
In my search for teachers true.
And from the throngs that crowd life's lanes,
With trust, I have selected you.
Now will you give him your total love?
Nor think the labor vain,
Nor hate Me when I come
To take him back again?
I know you'll give him tenderness
And love will bloom each day.
And for the happiness you've known!
Forever grateful stay.
But should I come and call for him
Much sooner than you'd planned
You'll brave the bitter grief that comes
And someday you'll understand.
For though I'll call him home to Me
This promise to you I do make,
For all the love and care you gave
He'll wait for you, inside Heaven's Gate.*

A kind person sent me the above poem when I lost my Joshua. I hope it speaks the truth - I hope he is waiting at Heaven's gate.

NEWFOUNDLAND DOG STORIES

The most famous Newfoundland dog stories invariably bring a tear to the eye. Most of us know that the Peter Pan dog was Luath, the Landseer Newfoundland owned by the author, J.M. Barrie, but other newfies have gone down in history for their loyalty, courage and endurance.

Let us not forget **Seaman**, the black newfoundland dog who went on the Lewis and Clarke Trail in the early nineteenth century.

This is the monument to Seaman which stands outside the Custom House in Cairo, Illinois.

Or **Gander,** who gave his life to save Canadian soldiers from a grenade thrown by the Japanese enemy.

Lord Byron's inscription on the tomb of his beloved Boatswain, is well known.

The Newfie has been famous throughout history for his courage and endurance, for his sweet, gentle nature, and for his loyalty.

The Landseer newfoundland got his name from the many paintings of the dog by Sir Edwin Landseer.

Many people have trained newfies as assistance dogs and one local one to me was reported as doing all the washing for his disabled owner. He would put the machine and detergent in the front-loading washing machine, switch it on and when it was finished, drag it out into a basket and load it into the dryer, which he also turned on. Once finished, he would unload it into a basket. Then he would help his wheelchair bound mistress to fold it. What an amazing dog!

In more recent years there has been **Bilbo,** the lifeguard newfie who works with the lifeguards on the coast of Cornwall, in the west of England.

SEAMAN, THE NEWFIE EXPLORER

In the early nineteenth century Seaman, a black Newfoundland Dog, was bought for $20 by Captain Meriweather Lewis and made his way across America on the first overland expedition.

This is the monument to Seaman which stands outside the Custom House in Cairo, Illinois.

It was an arduous journey, all the way from the Atlantic to the Pacific coast and during the journey the Newfie was bitten by a beaver, which bite severed an artery, and both Captains, Meriwether Lewis and William Clark, performed surgery to save the dog's hind leg.

In 1806, as they were preparing for their return trek home, the dog was stolen by Indians and Lewis sent three armed men to retrieve him.

The newfie's collar is in a museum in Virginia. The inscription on it reads: "The greatest traveller of my species. My name is SEAMAN, the dog of captain Meriwether Lewis, whom I accompanied to the Pacific ocean through the interior of the continent of North America."

The dog suffered much during that expedition, from almost losing his leg, having surgery with no anaesthetic, to being stolen by Indians and bitten by mosquitoes. He deserves his memorials.

He is now the official mascot of Lewis and Clark College's pioneers, and there are statues of him scattered across the United States.

Several books have been written about this famous dog, many non-fiction, as well as fiction stories based on fact. He will always be remembered.

By today's standards, I think it would be considered unacceptable to take a dog on such an arduous journey, but his adventures have immortalised him forever.

He is probably the most famous newfoundland dog in history.

GANDER, THE BRAVEST NEWFIE

Gander was a black Newfoundland Dog who was originally someone's pet, and named Pal.

He accidentally scratched a child's face and the owner gave him to the Royal Rifles, a regiment of the Canadian Army stationed at Gander International Airport, in Newfoundland.

The soldiers renamed the dog after the airport and he accompanied them to Hong Kong in 1941

The battle of Hong Kong began in December 1941, after the Japanese attack on Pearl Harbour.

During the battle, the Japanese soldiers threw a hand grenade at the Canadians. The dog retrieved it and rushed it toward the enemy, thereby being killed in the explosion.

It wasn't until 2000 that the heroic dog was at last awarded the Dickin Medal for his actions. This medal is an animal equivalent of the Victoria Cross and it was the first such award since 1949.

The citation reads:

For saving the lives of Canadian infantrymen during the Battle of Lye Mun on Hong Kong Island in December 1941. On three documented occasions, Gander, the Newfoundland mascot of the Royal Rifles of Canada, engaged the enemy as his regiment joined the Winnipeg Grenadiers, members of Battalion Headquarters "C" Force and other Commonwealth troops in their courageous defence of the island. Twice Gander's attacks halted the enemy's advance and protected groups of wounded soldiers. In a final act of bravery, the war dog was killed in action gathering a grenade. Without Gander's intervention, many more lives would have been lost in the assault.

His name is listed on the Hong Kong Veterans Memorial Wall in Ottawa, Canada, along with nearly 2000 men and women.

NEWFIE HISTORY

Newfoundland dog history begins on the island of Newfoundland off the East coast of Canada. This is a very ancient breed, which very likely originated in the region with the Vikings.

There is archaelogical evidence of the dog going back as far as the Vikings, and some theories involve outcrossing with the now extinct black wolf. What is clear is that the larger dog we have today evolved from the smaller St John Dog, who had a similar purpose.

The first time we see the name Newfoundland written in relation to a dog is in 1775, when sportsman and diarist, George Cartwright, gave the name of the island to his own dog.

In 1780 the Commodore-Governor of Newfoundland limited the ownership of the dog to one per household in some vain effort to promote sheep rearing, though I personally see little connection. It did nothing for sheep rearing, but did result in the breed almost becoming extinct.

Breed enthusiasts thankfully broke this law and continued to breed. In the eighteenth century the Newfoundland started to appear in literature such as Charlotte Bronte's Jane Eyre.

Records from 1824 indicate that there were 2000 of these dogs living and working on the island, pulling milk carts and hauling loads.

The dog has evolved with webbed feet. They are natural swimmers and have been famous for grabbing onto the ropes of sinking ships and hauling them back to shore. They have a natural instinct to rescue, and if they see anyone in distress in the water, they are likely to dive in, grab their arm and swim them to safety. They have also been known to dig people out of snowdrifts.

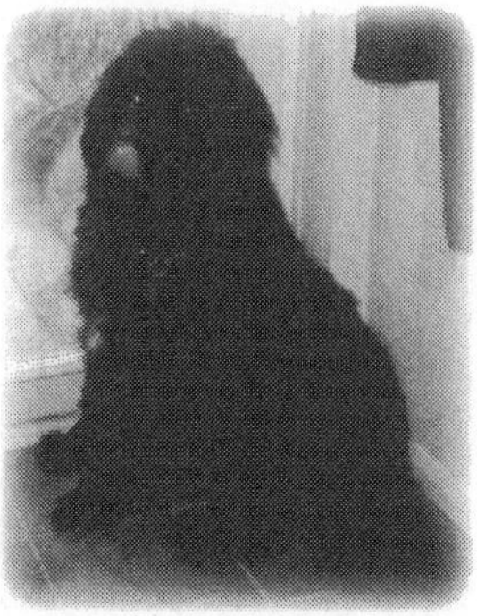

NEWFIE TRAINING

To understand how to start your newfoundland training, you need to also understand the history of these dogs and realise what they were bred for. Newfoundlands, like almost every giant breed, were bred to work independently of humans. They have been used in the past for many things, including pulling carts, but their main function has always been water rescue.

This inherent breeding makes them good pets, as they are naturally people friendly, but you have to remember that they will act on their own initiative if they think someone is in danger.

This independence means that they think of themselves as equals. They will not respond to harsh treatment; indeed such treatment can destroy their trust in you permanently. They will not respond to any outdated pack leader theories either. You are not his pack leader, he does not have a pack, you are his friend and the controller of all his resources.

The independent nature of the newfoundland dog gives him an edge in intelligence, but he will not work for free. Positive, reward based training is essential. If you want him to do something for you, he wants to know what is in it for him.

If you have an older newfie who has perhaps missed out on his basic puppy training it is not too late, though it will take much longer and will require more patience.

Find a high value treat that your newfie loves. Most newfies will do anything for food, and by a high value treat I mean something that he does not get all the time. He is not going to co-operate for a boring old dog biscuit!

You will need something different, pieces of chicken, pieces of cooked liver - many dogs love cheese, which is fine so long as it is given only as a treat and in small quantities. My dogs will do anything for liver cake (recipe in this book).

You will never force a newfie to do anything. They are easily frightened and they may never get over that fear. You do not work for no wages, why should he?

A nice high value treat, the second he does what you want, will get him interested and looking forward to the next command.

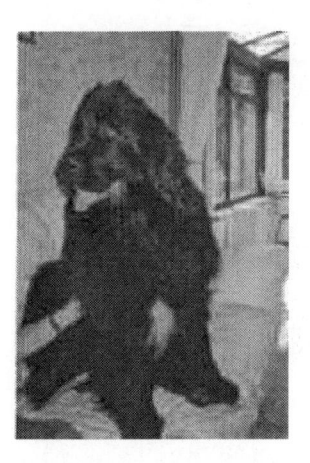

You need to build a relationship with your newfie so that he will do anything to please you. None of this is difficult, but it does take time and patience, especially if he has had no training. If you adopt a newfoundland dog from **Newfoundland Rescue** it is likely that you will have to start from scratch.

HOUSETRAINING

A Newfoundland puppy is easy enough to housetrain, but you have to teach him the right way from the beginning.

A Newfoundland puppy is an extremely intelligent dog and will understand what is required of him if the right approach is used.

The first thing to learn is the way that dogs think. They learn by association. It is no use yelling at him after he has gone in the wrong place - it is too late by then and he will associate your presence with being scolded. He has no idea what he is supposed to have done and showing him will not improve that situation.

All he will know is that you come home and he gets shouted at. So, do you want your Newfoundland puppy to come and greet you with his tail wagging? Or do you want him to run away and hide as soon as he hears you coming?

You need to watch him carefully, look for signs that he is sniffing around, looking for a place to go. As soon as you see this, you must pick him up and take him outside into the garden. Do not just leave him out there - he will forget about going and want to follow you inside. You need to stay with him, wait for him to go no matter how long it takes. You can associate a word with this, as soon as he performs, but not until.

You should also take him outside after he has eaten and when he wakes up. Puppies will toilet a lot. It is hard work keeping up with them, but it will not take long provided that you pay attention to every little move he makes.

Once he has toileted where he is supposed to give him lots and lots of praise and treats, then let him back inside.

What if he starts to go in the house? You simply pick him up and take him outside, even if it is too late and say nothing. He will not understand if you scold him for going in the house; he will think he is being scolded for doing what he must do. The result of this will be that he will either find somewhere to go where you cannot see him, or he will wait until you are out of the room.

In his mind, he gets scolded if you are there; he does not get scolded if you are not there, and you will have forfeited your chance to praise him for going in the right place. No way is he going to perform with you hanging about!

If he does toilet in the house, and it will happen on occasion, be sure to clean it thoroughly with a biological washing powder or one of the many products available from pet stores. If the smell still lingers, he is more likely to go in that spot again.

I managed to housetrain Ferdie in two days, but he was a little older at 13 weeks. We still had accidents at night of course, but they were always beside the back door, proving that he was first waiting for someone to let him outside.

It is a good idea to remove rugs and cover carpet with heavy plastic sheeting. This is easier to clean and will ensure that the smell does not linger.

The same principles apply with a full grown dog who has never been housetrained, perhaps living outside in kennels. The only difference is that you can't pick up a full grown newfoundland and put him outside! But you should still take him out so that he knows. It doesn't take long, it takes patience and paying attention.

Positive Dog Training

Positive dog training is the only way to reliably train your puppy or older Newfie, if you want his love and loyalty.

Training has come a long way in the past sixty years or so, so if you think you need to be your dog's pack leader, you need to rethink your own position and that of your dog. Unfortunately, some trainers still cling to this myth, at the expense of dogs and their welfare.

Back in the 1920's, a study was carried out using a group of unrelated, captive wolves. These brilliant researchers came up with the theory that there was an Alpha Male among the wolves, a leader to whom the others deferred.

They noticed that this "alpha" wolf always ate first and that he positioned himself higher than the others. This is where the daft idea of not allowing your dog on the sofa or bed came from - he mustn't be allowed to be higher than you. I even read once on a forum a man looking for advice because his 'knowledgeable' wife was afraid to sit down near her new, full grown Great Dane because if she sat he was higher than her! Unbelievable rubbish.

Since that time, it has been established that wolves do not live in packs which have a leader; they live in family units where the leaders are the parent couple. Once the cubs have grown they will go off and establish their own family unit, but in the meantime, when food is scarce, it is the babies who eat first, never the parents.

Unfortunately, despite much research to the contrary, this theory has embedded itself into our culture and we still have many so-called trainers spouting this nonsense about having to be your dog's pack leader, having to dominate him

This theory has not only been discredited, but the original researcher who came up with it has stated many, many times that he was wrong!

The first thing to remember is that dogs are not wolves anyway. They are thousands of years evolved from being wolves, they do not behave like wolves, they do not live in family units, and in the wild they will fight over resources such as food, shelter and females, never will they fight to establish their leadership.

This in turn means that whilst one dog might win the much sought after food, another might win the female. There is no defined leader

How many times have you read or seen on TV that the dog will think of you as part of his pack, and that you have to establish yourself as his pack leader? To do this you are supposed to go through doors first (how many doors does a wild dog need to open?) You need to always eat first (the dog isn't even noticing). You must not let him on the sofa! Well, how is he going to get on my lap and have a cuddle if he is not allowed on the sofa?

You may also have read or seen that your dog is trying to dominate you, that he is trying to dominate the door (no, he is just excited about visitors), he is trying to dominate you by squashing you up into the corner (no he is just after your cup of tea).

One of the silliest things I ever read was that if my dog puts both paws on my lap, he is being dominant! I would say he either wants a cuddle or he is trying to tell me something.

Dogs do not want to dominate humans.

The most damaging conclusion that came out of this original study is that the pack leader will pin another dog down, performing an "alpha roll" to let the other dog know who is boss. Pinning a dog down in this way will only intimidate and scare him into biting, as he sees this as his only defence.

They failed completely to notice that the dog positioned himself on his side or his back, as a sign of submission. This is something that a lot of dogs do as though he is saying "I don't want a fight, you win". No other dog is pinning him in this position and the idea of pinning your dog down to make him behave is extremely damaging, both mentally and emotionally.

Positive dog training is no different from the way people have been training wild animals for years. You would not put a shock collar on a whale, would you? Captive creatures like that will not perform tricks because some human threatens them - they will do it for rewards.

Dogs have a language all their own and it is subtle, easy for us mere humans to miss.

There are books that have been written by highly qualified experts, and they will help you to understand what your dog is actually saying. If you get his body language wrong, you will do yourself and your dog a lot of harm. Many highly qualified animal behaviourists have been studying canine behaviour for many years and they are all agreed on one thing – dogs are not pack animals. They are social creatures w who want nothing more than to be close to their humans and give them companionship. You will establish yourself as leader simply by being the one with the resources.

So, do Newfoundland dogs need special training? No. All dogs deserve to be trained using love, praise and rewards.

So what is positive dog training? It is the simple skill of giving something in return for something.

You need to build a relationship with your newfie so that he will do anything to please you. None of this is difficult, but it does take time and patience, especially if he has had no training. If you adopt a newfoundland dog from Newfoundland Rescue it is likely that you will have to start from scratch.

NEWFIE BREEDERS

Finding good newfoundland dog breeders is essential if you are thinking about a newfie puppy.

As newfoundlands become one of the most popular dog breeds, they are being bred more and more by puppy farmers and back yard breeders.

Just to be clear: A puppy farmer (or puppy mill) is one who will keep many different breeds of dog, usually in appalling conditions. These dogs will be kept outside in kennels with the bare minimum of comfort provided.

Their bitches are overbred. They no sooner have a litter and they are being mated once more to provide more puppies to sell to make more money. That is the prime consideration of a puppy farmer - money.

Their puppies will not be registered with kennel clubs. The UK Kennel Club states a maximum of six litters per bitch, but thankfully that is changing to four from next year.

Their dogs will not be vaccinated, so all sorts of horrible diseases can be passed on to the puppies.

The puppies will have had no health checks, no worming, no anything really and are very often sold off at 6 weeks or younger, which is a prime socialisation time for the puppy to learn from his littermates.

There will definitely be no health certificates. The parents' hipscores will not be taken before breeding, so your puppy could well end up suffering from hip dysplasia. No elbow scores or heart scans will have been taken either.

Back yard breeders can be much the same, only on a smaller scale.

Sometimes an owner will breed one litter from her bitch. There is an old wives' tale that it is good for a bitch to have one litter before being spayed, which is quite frankly, rubbish.

These people mean well, and could have very healthy puppies, but they should have those health tests done before breeding. It is vitally important in any dog, but in a newfoundland it is even more important.

None of the above are good newfoundland dog breeders

How to Avoid Puppy Farmers

Puppy farmers are easy enough to spot, if you do your homework.

- Never take a puppy that is under eight weeks of age.
- Never arrange to collect a puppy from a neutral location - the breeder does not want you to see their premises.
- Make sure you see all the puppies, in the house with their mother.
- Make sure you have their health certificates, their full pedigrees and their kennel club registration.
- Never buy from a pet store, no matter how reputable. They get their stocks from puppy farmers.
- If the breeder does not want you to visit before you collect your puppy, alarm bells should ring.
- Although many puppy farmers try to charge the same price as a good, health tested, puppy, be very suspicious if the puppy is a lot less than it should be.

In the United Kingdom, the average price of a newfoundland puppy from good lines is between £1200 and £1500 (as at 2014). Be very wary if the pups are much cheaper than that.

Good newfoundland dog breeders will want to meet you, will ask about your experience and circumstances, they will want to know how you are with their dogs.

When I first saw Ferdie, having been recommended to the breeder in question, he was 12 weeks old. He had been kept back because of a hernia, which they had already had fixed.

The breeder was perfectly honest about this, told me from the beginning that he was not to be used at stud as hernias can be passed on to puppies, told me there would be breeding restrictions on him. I just wanted a nice natured, big hairy dog, so those things did not bother me.

It was a little late to be collecting a puppy, but he had spent those extra weeks with his friends, and he was well socialised to all their other dogs. And I had experience of large dog breeds, though not as large as these.

I had to meet every adult dog they had before seeing him. Yes, they probably wanted to show off their beautiful, champion dogs, but it also gave them the opportunity to see how I reacted to dogs of this magnitude. All these things were signs of a good newfoundland dog breeder.

How to Find Good Newfoundland Dog Breeders

A good breeder will breed their dogs to preserve and improve the breed. Although they have to cover their expenses, and health tests are very expensive, they are more interested in the puppy's welfare than they are in the money.

Ferdie's breeder could not have made anything on him, as they had paid for all his injections, had him microchipped and paid for his medical treatment. Then they gave me a discount, because I didn't ask for one! There were two other people interested in him, and both had wanted a discount because of his hernia operation. I had fallen deeply in love with him and would not have cared if they wanted more.

The first place to start is the breed club. There are Newfoundland breed clubs all over the world, and they will always advise you as to what you are taking on, and provide you with the name of a good breeder. They have nothing to gain by this freely given information, except to contribute to the welfare of the dogs. They do not want to see another Newfie end up in rescue.

The United Kingdom Newfoundland Club can be found at **Newfoundland Club**

In the United States there are several branches but this is the best place to start **Newfoundland Club of America**

In Canada start at **Newfoundland Club of Canada**

In New Zealand **Newfoundland Club of New Zealand**

If you live in the United Kingdom, a well respected site for finding a reputable breeder is Champdogs. On the Champdogs site you can view your puppy's pedigree. Look for ancestors typed in red - these are champion dogs. You may have to go on a waiting list for a puppy. Breeders of this calibre do not breed all the time and they usually have a waiting list for their puppies. Try not to be impatient, it will be the best thing in the long run. A really good puppy is worth waiting for.

You have decided on a newfoundland puppy, you are excited, can't wait, and you want him now! Trust me, it is not worth it. You may be lucky enough to find a good breeder who has a puppy left; it happens. Sometimes their buyer changes their mind, circumstances change, but if that does not happen, do not rush into the next best thing. You will end up regretting it.

CHOOSING A PUPPY

Choosing a puppy is not something to be done impulsively. A lot of consideration must be given to this choice, do not let your heart rule your head.

As newfies become one of the most popular dog breeds, they will be bred more and more by puppy farmers and back yard breeders, trying to make a quick profit with no thought for the puppy's welfare, nor for the sort of home they are going to.

All they care about is the money.

This is Joshua at about five months old. See how healthy he looks? That is what your puppy should look like so try to remember that when choosing a puppy.

Your puppy must have three health certificates: elbow scores for both parents, hip scores for both parents, and heart scans.

Elbow scores should be at zero or close to zero, hip scores should be under 25 and fairly even for both hips. The lower the hip score, the less chance of the dog developing **hip dysplasia**. Heart scans should provide evidence that there is no sign of **subvalvular aortic stenosis** in the puppy's history.

You should be able to see the litter of puppies in the breeder's house, with their mother

What is their mother like? Is she a friendly dog? Does she come to say hello, does she seem pleased to show off her puppies?

A good breeder will breed for temperament as well as health, so be sure that the mother is an approachable dog. Do not be fooled by being told that she is defensive of her pups - this is rarely the case.

The puppies should come to you willingly, not appear nervous but should be curious about you

If the breeder has young children in the house, watch for signs that the children have been allowed to pull the puppies around at will. This sort of treatment can result in a permanently nervous and sometimes aggressive dog.

You also need to see the puppy's pedigree and make sure no interbreeding has been going on.

Look carefully at the mother when choosing a puppy and preferably the father as well. Do they look like a Newfoundland dog is supposed to look like? Or do they look more like you wouldn't really know what breed they are?

Try to see the father as well. If he is not available, and you are buying a male puppy, it is advisable to meet a full grown male dog. Newfoundland females are a lot smaller than the males, so be sure you are prepared for that when choosing a puppy.

A good breeder will not allow a puppy to leave its litter until it is at least eight weeks old, sometimes ten weeks. This is because a puppy needs to be with his littermates where he will learn bite inhibition and other dog language which you will find it difficult to teach.

A responsible breeder will not sell a puppy just before Christmas unless they know you very well or have special references for you. They are always wary of people trying to buy a puppy as a Christmas present for someone who may not be prepared to have a dog, and may not really want one. People seem to think a puppy would be a good present for their little nephew or niece, may have heard someone in the family say that they like newfies. That doesn't mean that they really want one or would know how to care for one. Good breeders are extremely careful about this sort of thing.

Christmas puppies also suffer from the time of year, the excitement, the noise. A puppy must be kept quiet for his first few days in his new home and Christmas is not the time to do this.

Would you believe that I once read a forum post by a breeder of Red Setters who said that someone had wanted to have one of her puppies, just for over Christmas, because he was red and would look nice in the photographs! This is the sort of mentality breeders have to deal with, so do not be offended if your chosen breeder will not allow any of their puppies to go just before Christmas.

A good breeder will also ask you lots of questions. They will want to know if you have experience of dogs, how much experience, what sort of house you have, are you at work all day?

Do not be offended by these questions - they are a sign of a caring breeder.

They may be reluctant to sell a puppy of this magnitude to a first time dog owner and they may refuse to sell to someone who is at work all day.

A good breeder will also tell you that if, for any reason, you cannot keep the dog, they will take him or her back, no matter what age he is.

They will want to meet you and have you see the puppies when they are about four weeks old. This is for your benefit as well as theirs, as you can assess the situation and get to know the breeder while they get to know you. It is well worth doing, even if you have to travel a long way to do it. But do not be surprised if there is a waiting list and you have to wait for the next litter.

Things to Beware of

Do not find your puppy in the free ads or on internet sites. Be very suspicious if the puppies are not kept in the house in a proper birthing pen. They should not be outside in a kennel. No good breeder would keep their puppies that way.

Never buy a puppy from a pet store, no matter how reputable. They get their stocks from puppy farmers.

Be very suspicious if the price is too low. The price of a Newfoundland puppy from a good breeder in the United Kingdom will be in the region of £1200 to £1500. If the price is much lower than that, you need to wonder why.

I was once asked for advice by someone whose friend was thinking of buying from an ad she had seen in the free ads internet site. The owners were advertising a litter of Landseer newfoundland puppies for £750 each, which I knew was much too cheap. I emailed them enquiring about the parents' hip scores and heart scans, pretending to be interested. I got no reply, which tells me that no health checks had been carried out. The friend was convinced, however, not by this evidence of a poor litter, but by my telling her that Ferdie is 80kg. The usual exclamation of "I didn't know they got *that* big" was her reply. It makes one wonder what people think giant breed actually means.

You may think you are getting a bargain. You are not. You will end up paying a lot more in vet bills and heartache in the long run.

Unfortunately, it is human nature to feel they have got a bargain. I have lost count of the number of people who have told me, very smugly, that they have seen newfie puppies much cheaper than I paid for mine. They seem to think that I will feel that I have been conned, but I know better.

And it is just this attitude which keeps the puppy farmers and back yard breeders in business.

There is no such thing as a bargain when it comes to buying a puppy and if you are thinking mostly about the price, then perhaps it is not the right time to have a puppy.

Of course, some puppy farmers and backyard breeders try to sell their unhealth tested puppies at top pedigree prices, so all things need to be considered.

Run away, very fast, if the breeder wants to meet you in a neutral location to hand over a puppy. That is always a sign of a puppy farmer who does not want anyone to see their premises.

Try to find out all you can on the phone. Once you have seen these cute little fluffy puppies, it is very often the hardest thing in the world to walk away if things don't feel right.

So how do you find a good breeder? Contact the breed club. There are Newfoundland Clubs all over the world who will give you the names of reputable breeders and further advise you on what to look for.

NEWFIE HEALTH

Your Newfoundland Dog health is an important factor to consider when you set out to share your life with this beautiful dog.

He may look robust, but the fact is that all large dog breeds are prone to certain conditions, which you must watch out for.

Newfoundland Puppies

Your puppy will need vaccinations against some nasty diseases before he can be let on the ground where other dogs may have been. If introducing a puppy into a home where there is already an older dog, make sure that the adult dog has his vaccinations up to date. Outside is different, as you have no idea what dogs have been there before.

Your puppy must be vaccinated at between seven and eight weeks of age, whilst he still carries some immunity from his mother. Many breeders will give the first vaccination before the puppy goes to his new home, but you must make sure that this has been done. If you are collecting your puppy at eight weeks however, it is not unusual for the breeder to expect you to arrange all vaccinations. You will need to carry him into the vets to protect him and be sure to tell the vet that it is a first vaccination.

Vaccinations need to include **canine parvovirus**, **canine hepatitis**, leptospirosis, **canine distemper** (also known as hard pad) and **kennel cough**.

If you do not live in one of the countries that have eliminated the disease, you should also have your puppy vaccinated against **canine rabies**.

Your puppy's second vaccination should be carried out two weeks later, at the age of ten weeks, and it should be a further week before you can safely take him outside.

If you have bought an older puppy, be sure he gets that first vaccination as soon as possible. After that, the same waiting periods apply in order to give the vaccination time to work.

It is a good idea to find a good vet before you get your puppy home. Ask your friends and neighbours who have animals what their vet is like. If you don't have that advantage, visit them all and ask to meet the vet in charge.

Unfortunately, not all vets are animal lovers. In my experience, a lot seem to be only in it for the money and you want someone who cares about your dog's welfare as much as you do.

Your puppy also needs to have flea treatment and to have been wormed. The first worming is usually done by the breeder, but do remember to ask.

Newfoundland puppies and adult dogs are particularly prone to **heat stroke** in the summer months. I nearly lost Joshua at only ten weeks old from heatstroke, yet he was only in the house with Ferdie. The symptoms of this started as him stumbling, vomiting, unable to drink. My vet saved his life and he wasn't too proud to ask advice from the vet school.

CANINE PARVOVIRUS

Canine parvovirus, or simply parvo, is spread through direct or indirect contact with faeces. Since the disease can remain in the soil for many months, your puppy must be vaccinated before his little feet can be allowed to touch the ground.

Very young puppies are often unable to have the vaccination, as they still carry an immunity from their mother which will clash with the vaccine. Buying your puppy from anything other than a good, responsible breeder will increase the risk of him contracting this disease, as it is unlikely that puppy farmers will bother to vaccinate their dogs. Do lots of research into the breeder before **choosing a puppy** to reduce the risk of this heartbreaking disease.

There are two types of the disease, intestinal and cardiac. A dog with the intestinal strain will exhibit signs of vomiting and bloody diarrhea. A dog with the cardiac type will have respitory and cardiovascular problems.

Puppies are far more susceptible to this disease than adult dogs, and if left untreated it has a 90% mortality rate.

If you think your puppy or dog may have contracted this virus, take him to the vet immediately and take his advice. Treatment is available, but it must be administered at once.

Be aware that the virus can remain on your floors and on your clothing for many months. Thoroughly clean all floors and carpets and wash clothes. Also inform your neighbours who have dogs; knowledge could prevent their dogs from getting the disease.

Your puppy will be weaker for 8 to 12 weeks after he has recovered from the illness and his immune system will not be able to fight normal infections. He will need careful monitoring during this time to ensure that he does not contract anything else.

CANINE HEPATITIS

Canine hepatitis affects the liver, kidneys, lungs and eyes of a dog.

It is spread through direct contact with the faeces and saliva of infected dogs. Sometimes it can result in death within hours of the first symptoms appearing.

Symptoms including fever, vomiting, diarrhoea, coughing, stomach pain and pale gums. Conjunctivitis can also occur. Dogs who have recovered from this disease can develop a clouding of the eye, but this usually clears up over time.

The disease is highly contagious and the dogs who have recovered are still infectious to other dogs for a period of six months or more.

Vaccination is the only real prevention of this horrible disease and that can convey immunity for up to three years.

Hepatitis is just one of the painful and life threatening illnesses your puppy can easily pick up. Make sure that he is vaccinated against this as well as the other diseases mentioned on this site.

Leptospirosis (Weil's Disease)

Leptospirosis is spread through contact with the urine of infected dogs. It can also spread to humans.

There are two types of the disease, Leptospira icterohaemorrhagiae (Weil's disease) which is normally spread by the urine of rats. This disease can be contracted through direct contact, or from swimming in water that has been urinated in by infected rats.

Symptoms for this form of the illness can range from mild lethargy to more severe symptoms such as abdominal pain and liver damage. It can cause sudden death.

The second form of the disease, Leptospira canicola, is spread through the urine of infected dogs. A dog that has recovered from the disease can still spread it via their urine.

This latter form of the disease can cause kidney failure and can be fatal.

Although the disease is treatable, treatment is not always effective and sometimes involves blood transfusions. Treatment always involves anti-biotics.

It is vitally important that your puppy is fully vaccinated against the disease before being allowed out into the world, where infected dogs and rats may have urinated.

This is just one of the horrible, life-threatening diseases from which your puppy must be vaccinated. The disease is easily contracted, so the utmost care must be taken to prevent your puppy from contact with it.

CANINE DISTEMPER - HARD PAD

Canine distemper, also known as hard pad, is spread by close contact with an infected dog. It can cause mild symptoms, such as lethargy, and in other dogs it can prove fatal.

Dogs most at risk are those less than one year old, although it can still be contracted by any dog with a weakened immune system.

Symptoms include signs of a cold, runny nose and eyes, and coughing. This will be followed by vomiting and diarrhoea. As the disease progresses, a hardening of the dog's pads (hard pad) and possibly his nose as well, will appear.

A blood test will confirm severe reduction in the white blood cells of the affected animal.

Intravenous fluids are sometimes given to reduce dehydration after vomiting and diarrhoea, but there is no real cure for this disease and it can be fatal.

The only way to deal with this horrible disease is to prevent it happening in the first place, by vaccinating your puppy before he goes outside, except in your own garden.

Whilst early **socialisation** is important for your puppy's social development, remember that hard pad is contracted from close nose to nose contact with an infected dog. Whilst your puppy should see other dogs, it is vital that they do not get too close until they are fully vaccinated.

KENNEL COUGH

Kennel cough is a common disease which is caused by close proximity to dogs who are, or who have been infected.

It is extremely common in the summer months, when dogs go into kennels whilst their owners are away on holiday. Because of all the dogs together, there is invariably an outbreak of this disease.

Symptoms include harsh, dry coughing, tiredness and loss of appetite. Occasionally the illness can progress to pneumonia.

Treatment may include cough suppressants to alleviate the symptoms and antibacterials to relieve the disease, though these will not eliminate the infection.

It is not uncommon for a dog to contract kennel cough at sometime in his life, and although it is rarely fatal, infectiousness can last for several weeks after recovery.

If you suspect that your dog has contracted the disease, immediate veterinary treatment is essential to alleviate suffering. You need to tell everyone whose dogs he has been in contact with. You must also keep him away from other animals for some weeks afterwards.

The disease can spread to other animals, including cats and horses.

There is now a nasal vaccination against this horrible disease, which involves drops into the nostrils, rather than an injection. This vaccination can be given to a dog of any age and it is safe for puppies as young as three weeks.

Ensure that your puppy has these drops to keep him safe from this nasty disease.

CANINE RABIES

Canine Rabies has been eliminated in the United Kingdom. No cases of the disease have been found in the UK since 1902 and the last reported case from animals being brought into the country was in 1946.

The very word "rabies" fills one with fear. Because I live in the UK, I have never seen a real live case of this disease, but I do know that it will turn a normally placid and gentle dog into a killer.

Most countries, though, still have to be careful of their dogs catching the disease, which is almost always fatal and can be spread between dogs and other species, including humans.

The disease is spread by the bite or saliva of an infected animal. Early symptoms include irritation of the affected area, fever, change in behaviour and dilated pupils. However symptoms will not begin to show for at least four weeks after infection. The second phase of the infection causes aggression, disorientation and sensivity to light.

The final phase is paralysis, respiratory failure, hydrophobia (fear of water) and death.

Rabies is a killer, both of animals and humans. Any mammal can contract the disease, but it is normally carried by wild animals such as bats, racoons and wolves.

If you do not live in one of the countries which have eliminated this disease, be sure that your puppy is vaccinated.

Newfoundland Dog Health - Adult Dogs

Your growing or adult dog can still be susceptible to **canine hip dysplasia.**, even if his parents' hipscores are the best they can be. Remember that very little exercise should be the norm for a growing giant breed, but even an adult dog of this size can later develop hip or **elbow dysplasia** and you will need to watch out for signs of limping.

Subvalvular aortic stenosis is a heart disease for which Newfoundlands are particularly prone. You must have heart scan certificates from your breeder but if you do not, and even if you do, ask your vet to check for heart murmurs.

All giant dogs carry a risk of **canine bloat**, also known as gastric torsion, and care should be taken to prevent this. Do not exercise your dog, even a short walk, within one hour before or after eating. Your Newfoundland dog should be fed as an adult twice a day or even three times in smaller portions.

There is also a risk of early onset **canine arthritis.** Almost all large dogs will develop arthritis when they get old, but giant breeds can sometimes get this debilitating disease at a young age. Although it is not common in Newfoundlands, my Joshua was diagnosed with arthritis in his wrists at the age of only 19 months. I was very careful to limit his exercise whilst he was growing, but he contracted the illness anyway.

Special care must be taken with a growing puppy.

Supplements such as glucosomine and chondroitin, as well as Omega 3, are a great aid for alleviating joint problems. I have found from experience, though, that **dog hydrotherapy** has been the best treatment for Joshua's arthritis.

HIP DYSPLASIA

Canine hip dysplasia is a malformation of the hip joint, where the leg does not fit properly into the hip bone. The condition is usually hereditary, so it is essential that both parents of your puppy have low hip score certificates.

Although the condition is usually hereditary, there is a chance of it developing by too much exercise being allowed whilst the puppy is growing. It is essential to realise and provide the proper **puppy care** for this breed.

Symptoms include lameness, stiffness on getting up, sensitivity to touch and sometimes a marked change in behaviour. The dog will have great difficulty even climbing a small step.

The condition can only be diagnosed by x-rays and can be alleviated by supplements and anti-inflammatory medications, although sometimes this is not enough and surgery is required.

Surgery will involve the replacement of the hip joint, much as is done in humans. The procedure has had a great deal of success in dogs, but it is extremely expensive. Lifetime Insurance will cover this under normal circumstances. The recovery period is difficult in a dog, especially a young dog, and they will need to be kept fairly immobile whilst this is being achieved.

If left untreated the condition is crippling and can lead to severe **canine arthritis.**

Any indication of discomfort or pain should be investigated at the earliest opportunity.

All large dog breeds are susceptible to this condition and some have a much higher incidence of the condition than other breeds. A good breeder will never breed from a dog with a high hipscore. The average hipscore for a Newfoundland dog is 25, but a good hipscore will be far below that.

ELBOW DYSPLASIA

Elbow dysplasia in a dog occurs when the elbow joint, which is made up of cartilage and bone, is out of shape. This is when problems will occur. It is like a hinge, and if something gets in the way, it will not work properly.

Although the condition is normally hereditary, it can also be caused by arthritis setting in, getting in the way of the normal function of the elbow joint.

Dogs who have this condition will normally display signs at about six months of age. Symptoms will include lameness and possibly an uneven gait.

Treatment normally consists of supplements and limiting the dog's exercise. In severe cases, surgery may be required to remove bits of loose bone. Although there is no real cure, it is not a totally crippling condition and the dog can lead a reasonably normal life.

Because a Newfoundland dog is a fairly low energy dog, limiting exercise is not such a difficult task as it would be with a different breed.

It is essential that your puppy's parents have low elbow scores. 0 is the normal score, but slightly above, i.e. 1 is acceptable.

The condition can also be caused by too much exercise as a growing pup. The right sort of **puppy care** is essential to prevent this and other potentially crippling and painful conditions.

A dog with this condition is going to be in some pain and care should always be taken that he does not climb or overdo his running. Normally an intelligent dog like a Newfoundland will know when he has had enough, but it is still up to you to curb his enthusiasm.

Hydrotherapy is a wonderful treatment for joint problems of all kinds in a dog. It did more for my dog than anything else I have tried.

SUBVALVULAR AORTIC STENOSIS

Subvalvular aortic stenosis is the form of canine heart disease which is most common in the Newfoundland dog. It is an obstruction which causes a rushing noise in the blood as it passes through the valve. It manifests itself as a heart murmur.

Although parents should have heart scans before breeding it is not easily detectable and can show up in later generations. The parents may not necessarily have the disease, but can still be carriers.

Regular checks of a puppy are essential to detect any sign of heart murmur, as the murmurs can come and go and may not always be detectable. The puppy can appear absolutely normal in every other way.

X-rays and cardiograms are necessary to detect the condition, which can be controlled with drugs for the dog's lifetime, though it can never be completely cured.

Symptoms of heart failure include sudden lethargy, continuous heavy panting and a rise in temperature

Surgery has proved ineffective in dogs, unlike humans who have a good recovery rate.

The outcome of this disease is bleak, resulting in early cardiac arrest and sudden death.

You would treat a dog with canine heart disease the same as a human with a weak heart - gentle exercise, plenty of rest, and a careful watch on the dog's weight. He will not be able to run and play like any other dog, but he does not know that so it is up to us humans to provide him with the right care.

This disease is more likely to occur in certain breeds, but the Newfoundland dog has the highest incidence among giant dogs. It is essential that your puppy's parents have no sign of this condition in themselves and in their history.

CANINE BLOAT aka Gastric Torsion

Canine Bloat, or dog bloat, is the biggest killer of large dog breeds, second only to cancer. The awfulness of the condition is in its rapidity - it can kill a dog in less than an hour, long before medical treatment can be sought.

Prevention is the best thing. Never exercise your dog before or after a meal, even a short walk. Leave at least an hour either side, more if possible.

Newfoundland dogs should be fed is smaller portions of two or even three meals per day to reduce the risk of bloat. Never, ever let them get at the feed sack and eat the lot. Always keep it well locked up somewhere the dog cannot get at.

Symptoms include restlessness, unsuccessful attempts at vomiting, heavy panting, lying or standing with the back legs slightly splayed. There may also be a hardening of the stomach.

Not all symptoms will appear at once, however, so it is vital to pay attention to even one of these. The dog may also be drinking excessively.

Make sure you always have the number of an emergency vet, just in case.

It was always advised to raise the food bowl of a large dog so that he is not reaching down for his food. I was advised when I bought Ferdie to do this, and I have done so ever since, but recent research has suggested that the opposite is true and that a raised food bowl will actually cause bloat.

It is a subject that has cause heated argument and opinions are split. If you are going to get a Newfoundland dog, then you need to investigate and decide for yourself. I shall carry on with my raised bowls, as I have never had an incidence of the condition, but I will not advise anyone to do the same. This is something you need to make up your own mind about.

Just remember that bloat must be treated immediately or death will occur. Never think it is safe to wait till the morning and see how he is; it could be too late by then. Any one of the symptoms should be classed as an emergency, even if it turns out to be something else altogether.

CANINE ARTHRITIS

Canine arthritis is a heartbreaking condition, but one expects it to appear in an older dog, especially in a large dog breed.

It is particularly devastating, for both the owner and the dog, when it appears at a young age. There is no cure for arthritis in dogs, only medications and supplements to alleviate the condition. However, some success has been achieved with joint replacement surgery, much as is done in humans. This is a very expensive procedure, running into thousands of pounds, so lifetime insurance cover is an essential part of owning a newfoundland dog.

If the condition strikes in the hips or back legs, it can be possible under certain circumstances to replace the joints, but the disease in the front legs, as Joshua has, is more difficult because of the sheer weight of these dogs. The recovery time and care will also be stressful, especially for a young dog.

X-rays are needed to diagnose the disease effectively, then a course of anti-inflammatories can be given. The body produces glucosomine and chondroitin naturally, but the disease reduces the amount naturally produced. Without the addition of these supplements, my Joshua would not be able to walk. However, I have found that hydrotherapy is the best treatment to alleviate the condition. Your insurance policy may provide cover for this, so check carefully when you take out your insurance.

Leg tremors in a newfoundland dog can indicate arthritis. However, it is more likely to be growing pains, which many giant breeds do get because of the speed with which they grow. This is something they will grow out of when they reach maturity, but it is still advisable to get a vet to check these symptoms.

Early signs of the disease are limping, stiffness in getting up and excessive licking of the affected area.

DOG HYDROTHERAPY

For many years, humans have been discovering the benefits of swimming as exercise for damaged joints. In recent years it has been found that dogs can benefit just as much, if not more.

Hydrotherapy is often included in your dog's insurance, so check carefully. An insurance company may have a list of approved hydrotherapists which you will need to stick to if you want them to pay.

A lot of hydrotherapists will not see your dog without a referral from your vet, but all of them will want your vet to sign a form to say that the dog is healthy enough to swim.

In the UK they will be full members of the Canine Hydrotherapy Association. Just as not everyone can walk a dog efficiently, not everyone can swim a dog efficiently!

HEAT STROKE

Heat stroke in dogs can kill a dog in a very short space of time. Newfoundland dogs are particularly prone to this condition because of their heavy coats and their breeding, which is designed for cold climates.

Newfoundlands very often die very quickly when left in cars, and it doesn't even need to be particularly warm weather for the dogs to suffer.

I never leave my dogs in my car for more than a couple of minutes, no matter what the weather. Even then, I leave all the window wide open and I never lock it. I would rather risk someone stealing something than that my dogs should suffer; at least like that if something goes wrong, anyone can get them out.

When my Joshua was only ten weeks old, he developed heat stroke. He was in the house with Ferdie, and it was a particularly hot day.

First he began vomiting, then staggering about as though he could not get his balance. At only ten weeks, I was naturally quite frantic, but since he had received his booster vaccination the day before, I believed it was a reaction to that.

I rushed him to the vet, who took his temperature and diagnosed heat stroke. This little pup spent the next five hours sitting in a paddling pool at the vet's surgery, with a drip in his arm.

This horrible experience taught me one important lesson. Never wait and see how things will progress. Had I waited till the following day, I would have lost my lovely little puppy.

Always consult a vet straight away.

LIVER CAKE

Liver cake is a very simple recipe - even I can make it, and I never make cakes for the human inhabitants of the house!

300g liver
300g self raising flour
2 eggs
1 clove garlic (or tablespoon ground garlic)
water / milk

Put the liver and flour plus garlic in a blender, whizz until like a thick paste. Put the eggs in a jug, add same volume of milk or water (I use water). Add the egg mixture to the blender and whizz some more until smooth. Pour into baking tins, bake 30-45 mins at about 180 centigrade.

Turn out of tins, divide into portions (makes about 8-10 good sized portions) and freeze until needed.

Warning: if your blender starts to struggle, you will find that bits of tissue from the liver are wrapped around the blades...remove these and carry on!

Further Warning

Before it is actually cooked, liver cake stinks! Choose a day when you can open all your windows!

All temperatures are centigrade

LIVESTOCK GUARDIAN DOGS

I just wanted to say a few words about livestock guardian dogs, often referred to as LGDs. Unfortunately, these dogs are becoming more and more popular as domestic pets and believe me they are no such thing. All giant breeds have been bred to do a job and with dogs like newfoundlands and St Bernards that job has been rescue. That makes them naturally people friendly and accommodating, although they need to be given respect for their intellect.

Most giants, though, are livestock guardians. They have been bred to live with their flock, be it sheep, goats or cattle. They are introduced to the flock at a very early age, perhaps only four weeks, and they have a natural ability to protect that flock. They will defend it from all sorts of predators, from wolves to cheetah and this inbred ability makes them very suspicious of strangers.

If kept in a domestic situation, they think of their family and all the other pets as their flock and are suspicious of strangers. People have found that their children cannot have friends round because the dog sees the strange child as a threat. They are beautiful and intelligent dogs, but they are only pets if you have the isolated quantity of land for them and you understand them.

There are many breeds of livestock guardian and the only one which has so far been successfully domesticated, and that over centuries, is the Pyrenean Mountain Dog. Even they have been known to become quite out of control as they reach adulthood.

It seems too many people are seeing dogs as some sort of status symbol and are buying these beautiful creatures just to be different, when they know nothing about them.

The best giants to have as pets are newfies, Great Danes, St Bernards, Bernese Mountain Dogs, Greater Swiss Mountain Dogs. Sighthounds like the greyhound can make good pets, but remember they are likely to chase and kill smaller animals.

Just a word of warning. Never buy a dog for the wrong reasons and their appearance is the wrong reason.

On the next page is a picture of my Diva with a 10 week old Bernese Mountain dog - aren't they just adorable?

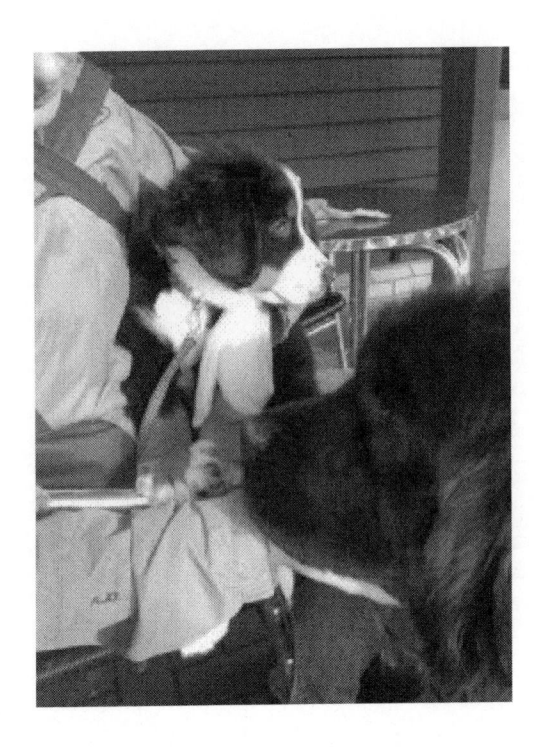

THE END

Copyright Margaret Brazear 2014-06-22

www.gentle-newfoundland-dogs.com

Printed in Great Britain
by Amazon